Latin HANON

30 Lessons for the Intermediate to Advanced Pianist

by Peter Deneff

ISBN 978-1-70512-169-6

Visit Hal Leonard Online at
www.halleonard.com

Contact Us:
Hal Leonard
7777 West Bluemound Road
Milwaukee, WI 53213
Email: info@halleonard.com

In Europe contact:
Hal Leonard Europe Limited
42 Wigmore Street
Marylebone, London, W1U 2RN
Email: info@halleonardeurope.com

In Australia contact:
Hal Leonard Australia Pty. Ltd.
4 Lentara Court
Cheltenham, Victoria, 3192 Australia
Email: info@halleonard.com.au

About the author

© David Yeh

Peter Deneff grew up in a musical home, exposed to classical music, Greek songs, and the Beatles. After several years of classical piano lessons with Leaine Gibson, he began jazz studies with the world-renowned pianist and David Bowie band member, Mike Garson. During this time he also studied many ethnic styles that influenced his composition and playing. He studied music composition and film scoring at California State University Long Beach, where he earned his Bachelors and Masters degrees in classical music composition. While at CSULB, Deneff composed his *Three Greek Dances for String Quartet*, which has been performed in the U.S., Canada, and Australia.

Peter has written many best-selling books for Hal Leonard, and has produced and recorded numerous arrangements for Yamaha, Hal Leonard, and PianoDisc. His original music and scoring was featured in the award-winning Charlie Sheen film, *Five Aces*. In 2012, Deneff composed the score for the feature film *Love of Life*. In early 2013, his involvement with the Hollywood animation community afforded him the opportunity to write the score for the short film *The Annies: 40 Year Retrospective,* which was presented as one of the highlights of the 2013 Annie Awards at Royce Hall, UCLA, and featured the legendary voice actress June Foray. Also, in 2013 Deneff scored the film *A Journey into the Holocaust*, produced by Paul Bachow.

Peter's stylistic versatility on the keyboard has allowed him to perform with a diverse assortment of artists such as Enrico Macias, Ebi, Tierra, Ike Willis (of Frank Zappa), Sonia Santos, Ramon Banda, Ritchie Garcia, Jerry Salas (of El Chicano), and Chalo Eduardo, as well as jazz greats Brandon Fields, Tom Brechtlein, Robert Kyle, Bruce Babad, and Bijon Watson.

Deneff's original project, Excursion, features mostly original works in a style best described as ethno-jazz. Excursion's sound is a blend of Brazilian, Cuban, Greek, Armenian, funk, classical, and progressive jazz. The group has been featured twice at the Playboy Jazz Festival and regularly performs at Herb Alpert's Vibrato Jazz Grill and the World Famous Baked Potato in Hollywood.

On the academic side, Peter has taught at Musician's Institute Hollywood, Orange County High School of the Arts, Cypress College, Fullerton College, and is currently an adjunct faculty member at Long Beach City College.

Acknowledgements

I would like to thank all the people in my life who have encouraged and supported me in my musical journey. My parents, George V. Deneff and Alkisti Deneff, my children, Gitana, George, and Sophia, and most of all, my wife, Diane, who continues to inspire, encourage and support me in my life and career. Lastly, I would like to thank all of the musicians and fans who continue to support me through my performances, recordings, and of course, enjoying my books!

Introduction

The study of Latin music is a broad and daunting endeavor for almost any musician. With its numerous sub-genres and country-specific musical conventions, a musician can easily be overwhelmed and confused as to where to start. Pianists are no exception. Being a rhythm section member as well as a melodic lead, piano players have a lot of ground to cover when it comes to learning how to play Brazilian, Cuban, Flamenco, and other Latin styles.

Specifically, the pianist must be rhythmically and technically capable enough to play montunos, (distinctive rhythmic motives that serve as a major driving force in some Caribbean music), they must have a certain grasp of jazz voicings, they must understand the comping styles of the various sub-genres, and they are often called upon to improvise in an idiomatically appropriate way. While this book does not attempt to address all of these stylistically, it does contain useful and fun material for developing the ability to physically execute various technical problems as they relate to Latin styles.

This book is intended as a sort of Latin sequel to Charles Louis Hanon's The Virtuoso Pianist in Sixty Exercises, a classic of piano literature that has been pushing pianists' technique to the limit for nearly 150 years. When this book is mastered, you will find that your technical prowess will be at a new level. The exercises in this book are perfect for either the beginner or the professional and can even benefit pianists of other genres such as jazz or classical. They may be practiced as quickly as they can be played cleanly and accurately. Some tips that I like to keep in mind when practicing these exercises include the following:

- Start very slowly, deliberately, and staccato. This builds articulation.
- Always use a metronome. The metronome will help you develop your sense of time and help you build velocity.
- When you master an exercise at a given speed, increase the tempo one notch on your metronome.
- Keep your fingers curved.
- Don't tense up.
- Push yourself, but stop if it hurts!

These exercises can and should be learned in all twelve keys (if they aren't already written that way) because it is important to feel at ease with any harmonic center. Mastering and being able to visualize chords and melodies in any key is vital to being a master pianist and improviser. You must learn all the "roads" of the keyboard so you don't ever get lost!

The main thing to remember is to have fun with these exercises, be creative, and find new ways to incorporate these techniques into your music, Latin or not. Last but not least, do not get discouraged. Technique doesn't happen overnight; it may take weeks or even months to master some of these exercises. It will certainly take longer to master them in all keys. Pace yourself, and you will succeed in mastering this book and be well on your way to becoming the next great Latin pianist!

Happy practicing,

Peter Deneff

1

2

3

4

5

6

26

7

28

30

8

34

9

10

11

12

50

52

13

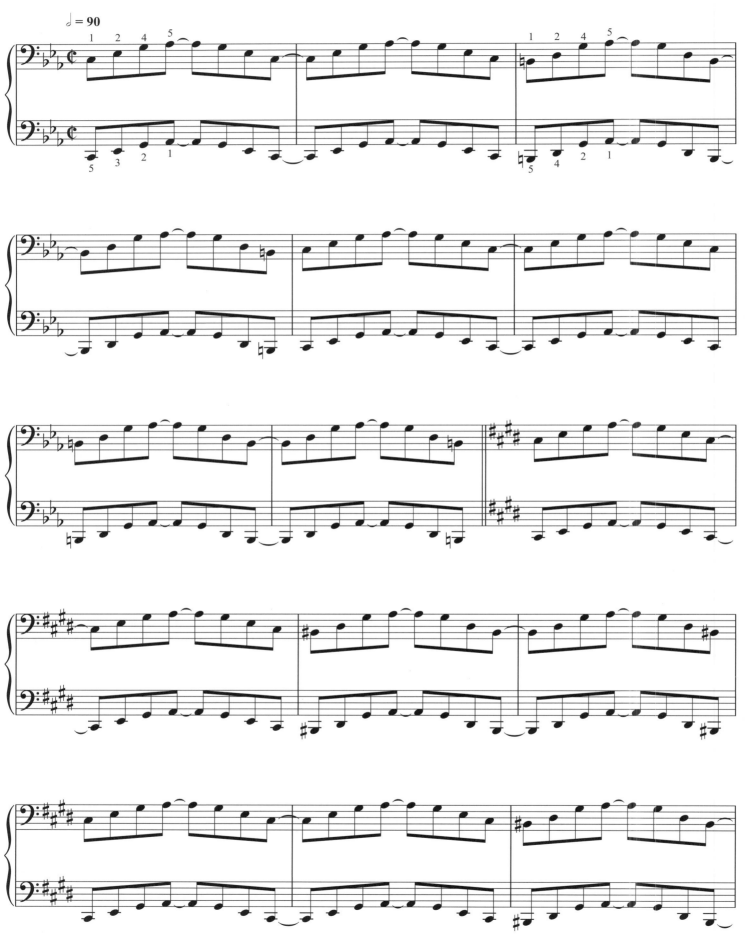

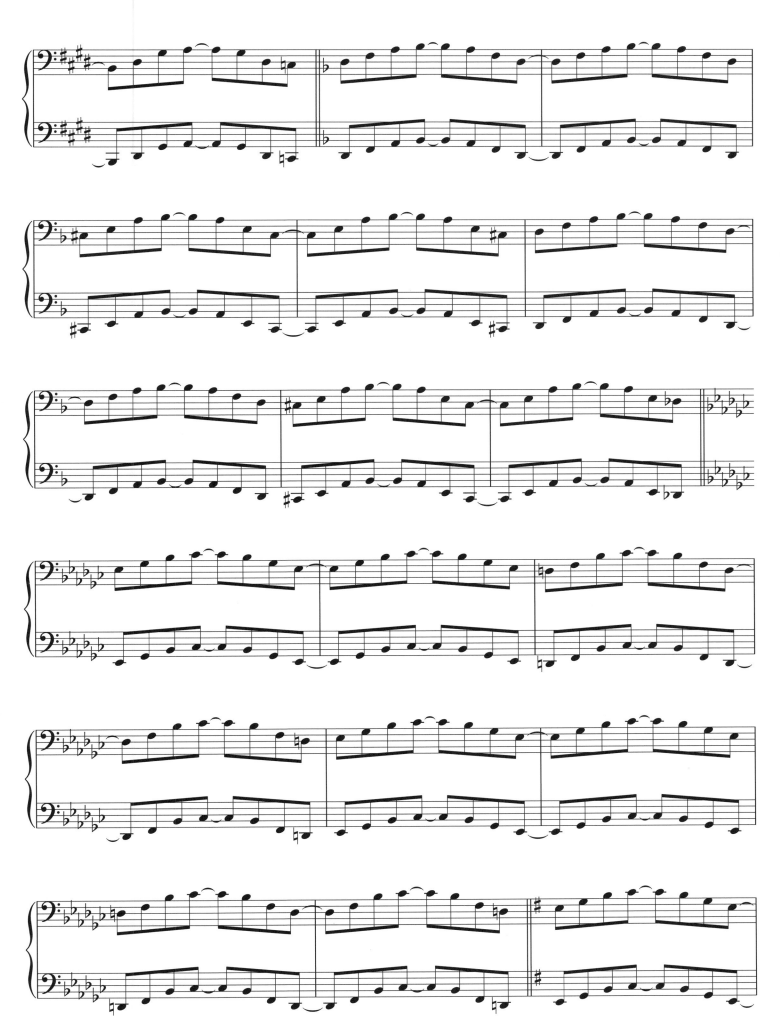

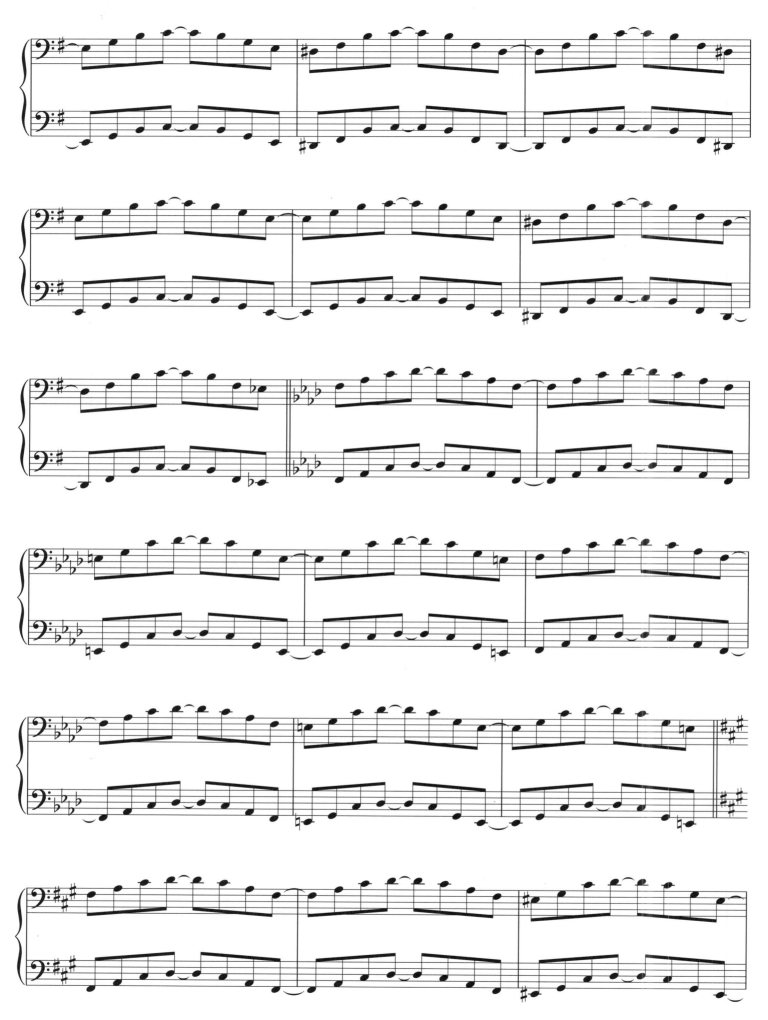

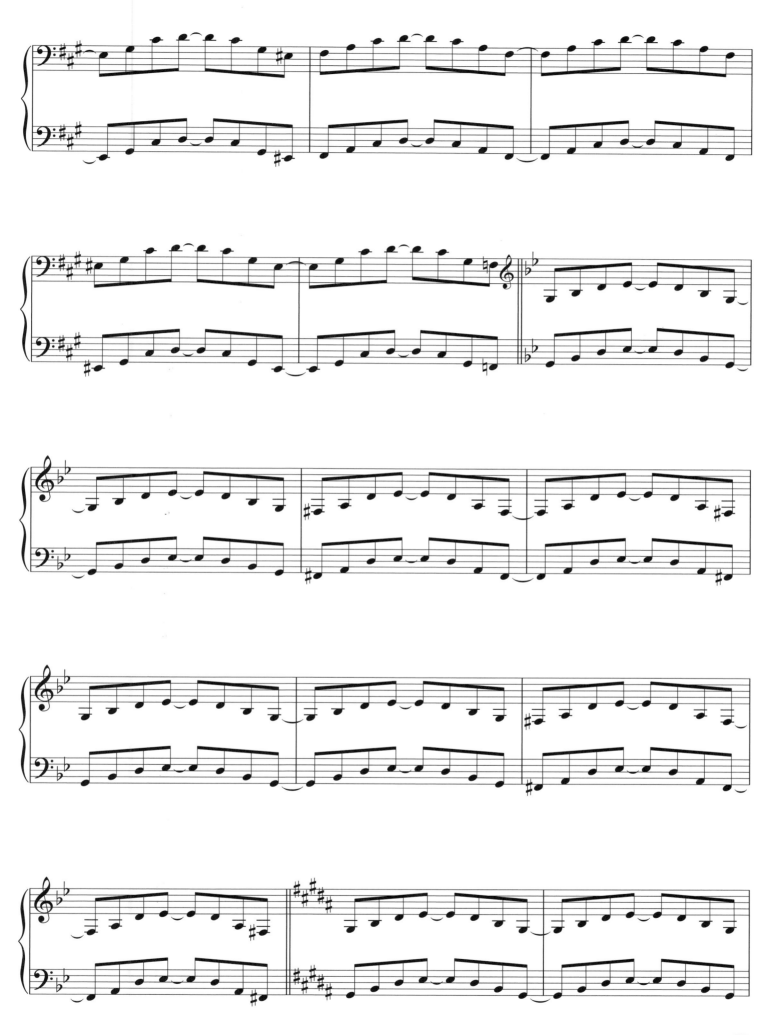

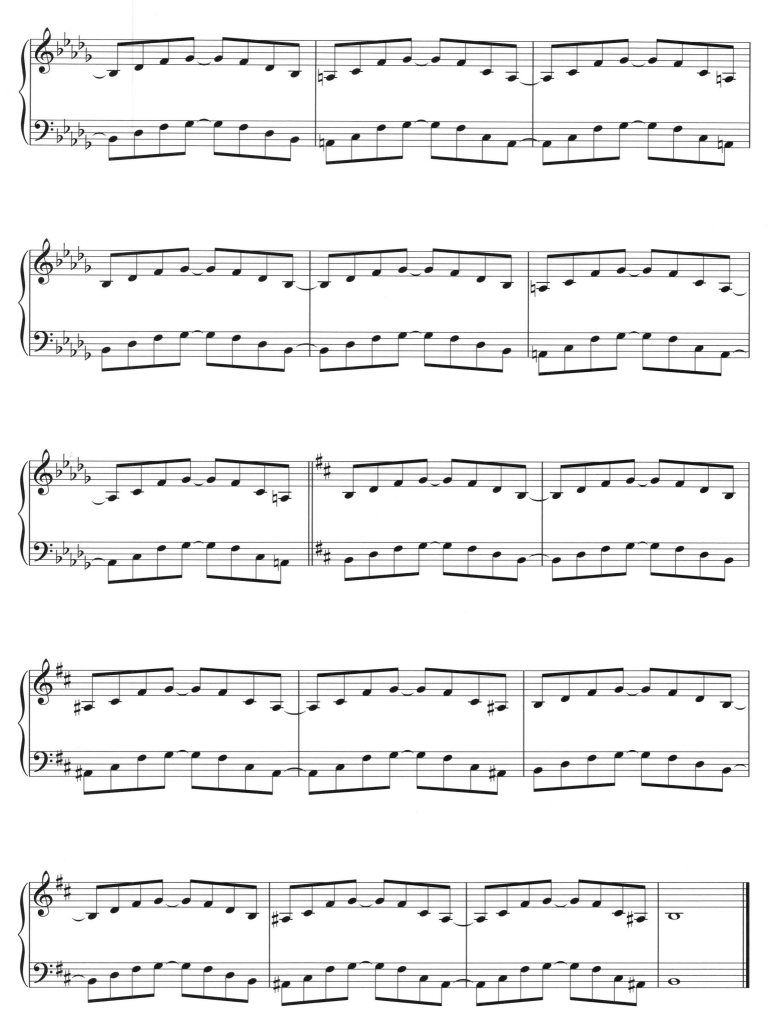

14

15

16

72

17

18

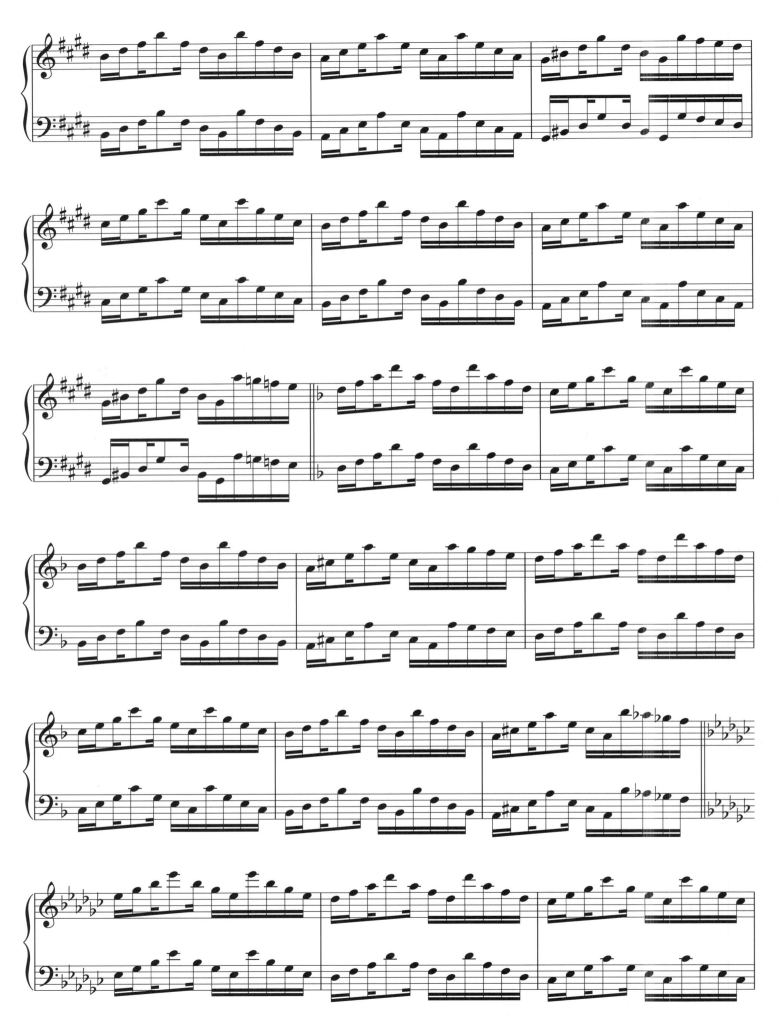

82

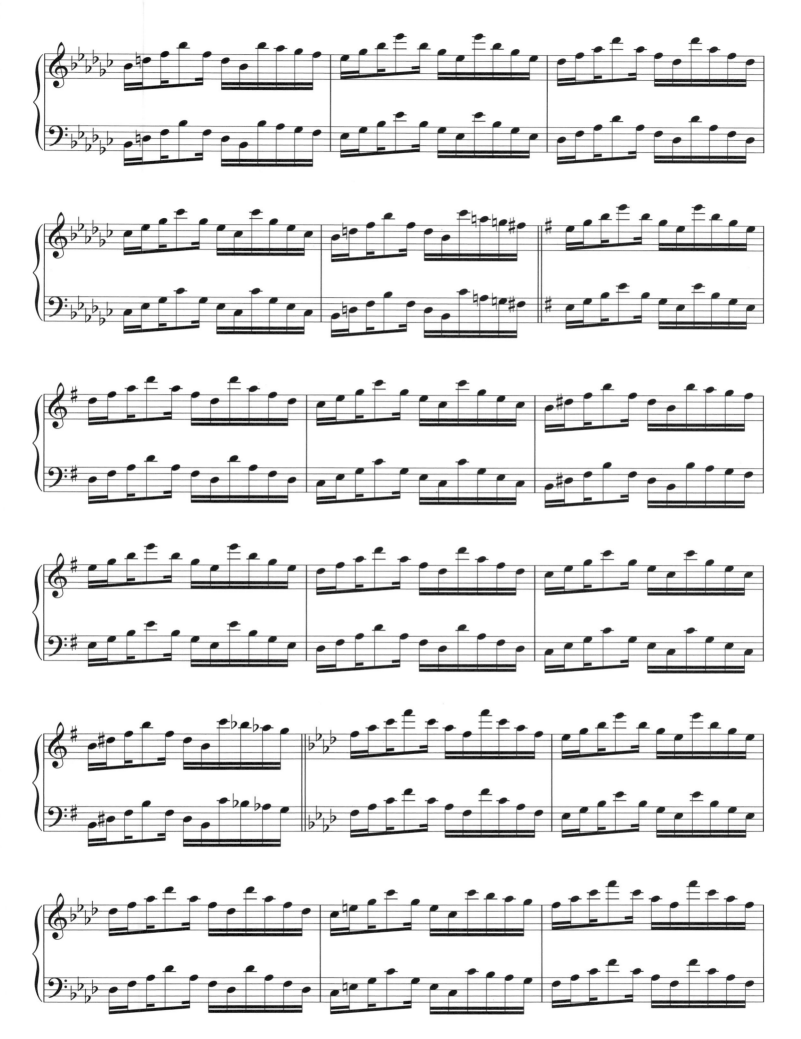

19

90

20

95

97

21

22

23

108

109

24

111

114

25

26

28

129

29

136

30

140

KEYBOARD STYLE SERIES

THE COMPLETE GUIDE!

These book/audio packs provide focused lessons that contain valuable how-to insight, essential playing tips, and beneficial information for all players. From comping to soloing, comprehensive treatment is given to each subject. The companion audio features many of the examples in the book performed either solo or with a full band.

BEBOP JAZZ PIANO
by John Valerio
This book provides detailed information for bebop and jazz keyboardists on: chords and voicings, harmony and chord progressions, scales and tonality, common melodic figures and patterns, comping, characteristic tunes, the styles of Bud Powell and Thelonious Monk, and more.
00290535 Book/Online Audio $18.99

BEGINNING ROCK KEYBOARD
by Mark Harrison
This comprehensive book/audio package will teach you the basic skills needed to play beginning rock keyboard. From comping to soloing, you'll learn the theory, the tools, and the techniques used by the pros. The accompanying audio demonstrates most of the music examples in the book.
00311922 Book/Online Audio $14.99

BLUES PIANO
by Mark Harrison
With this book/audio pack, you'll learn the theory, the tools, and even the tricks that the pros use to play the blues. Covers: scales and chords; left-hand patterns; walking bass; endings and turnarounds; right-hand techniques; how to solo with blues scales; crossover licks; and more.
00311007 Book/Online Audio $19.99

BOOGIE-WOOGIE PIANO
by Todd Lowry
From learning the basic chord progressions to inventing your own melodic riffs, you'll learn the theory, tools and techniques used by the genre's best practicioners.
00117067 Book/Online Audio $17.99

BRAZILIAN PIANO
by Robert Willey and Alfredo Cardim
Brazilian Piano teaches elements of some of the most appealing Brazilian musical styles: choro, samba, and bossa nova. It starts with rhythmic training to develop the fundamental groove of Brazilian music.
00311469 Book/Online Audio $19.99

CONTEMPORARY JAZZ PIANO
by Mark Harrison
From comping to soloing, you'll learn the theory, the tools, and the techniques used by the pros. The full band tracks on the audio feature the rhythm section on the left channel and the piano on the right channel, so that you can play along with the band.
00311848 Book/Online Audio $18.99

COUNTRY PIANO
by Mark Harrison
Learn the theory, the tools, and the tricks used by the pros to get that authentic country sound. This book/audio pack covers: scales and chords, walkup and walkdown patterns, comping in traditional and modern country, Nashville "fretted piano" techniques and more.
00311052 Book/Online Audio $19.99

GOSPEL PIANO
by Kurt Cowling
Discover the tools you need to play in a variety of authentic gospel styles, through a study of rhythmic devices, grooves, melodic and harmonic techniques, and formal design. The accompanying audio features over 90 tracks, including piano examples as well as the full gospel band.
00311327 Book/Online Adio $17.99

INTRO TO JAZZ PIANO
by Mark Harrison
From comping to soloing, you'll learn the theory, the tools, and the techniques used by the pros. The accompanying audio demonstrates most of the music examples in the book. The full band tracks feature the rhythm section on the left channel and the piano on the right channel, so that you can play along with the band.
00312088 Book/Online Audio $17.99

JAZZ-BLUES PIANO
by Mark Harrison
This comprehensive book will teach you the basic skills needed to play jazz-blues piano. Topics covered include: scales and chords • harmony and voicings • progressions and comping • melodies and soloing • characteristic stylings.
00311243 Book/Online Audio $17.99

JAZZ-ROCK KEYBOARD
by T. Lavitz
Learn what goes into mixing the power and drive of rock music with the artistic elements of jazz improvisation in this comprehensive book and CD package. This instructional tool delves into scales and modes, and how they can be used with various chord progressions to develop the best in soloing chops.
00290536 Book/CD Pack..$17.95

LATIN JAZZ PIANO
by John Valerio
This book is divided into three sections. The first covers Afro-Cuban (Afro-Caribbean) jazz, the second section deals with Brazilian influenced jazz – Bossa Nova and Samba, and the third contains lead sheets of the tunes and instructions for the play-along audio.
00311345 Book/Online Audio $17.99

MODERN POP KEYBOARD
by Mark Harrison
From chordal comping to arpeggios and ostinatos, from grand piano to synth pads, you'll learn the theory, the tools, and the techniques used by the pros. The online audio demonstrates most of the music examples in the book.
00146596 Book/Online Audio $17.99

NEW AGE PIANO
by Todd Lowry
From melodic development to chord progressions to left-hand accompaniment patterns, you'll learn the theory, the tools and the techniques used by the pros. The accompanying 96-track CD demonstrates most of the music examples in the book.
00117322 Book/CD Pack..$16.99

POST-BOP JAZZ PIANO
by John Valerio
This book/audio pack will teach you the basic skills needed to play post-bop jazz piano. Learn the theory, the tools, and the tricks used by the pros to play in the style of Bill Evans, Thelonious Monk, Herbie Hancock, McCoy Tyner, Chick Corea and others. Topics covered include: chord voicings, scales and tonality, modality, and more.
00311005 Book/Online Audio $17.99

PROGRESSIVE ROCK KEYBOARD
by Dan Maske
You'll learn how soloing techniques, form, rhythmic and metrical devices, harmony, and counterpoint all come together to make this style of rock the unique and exciting genre it is.
00311307 Book/Online Audio $19.99

R&B KEYBOARD
by Mark Harrison
From soul to funk to disco to pop, you'll learn the theory, the tools, and the tricks used by the pros with this book/audio pack. Topics covered include: scales and chords, harmony and voicings, progressions and comping, rhythmic concepts, characteristic stylings, the development of R&B, and more! Includes seven songs.
00310881 Book/Online Audio $19.99

ROCK KEYBOARD
by Scott Miller
Learn to comp or solo in any of your favorite rock styles. Listen to the audio to hear your parts fit in with the total groove of the band. Includes 99 tracks! Covers: classic rock, pop/rock, blues rock, Southern rock, hard rock, progressive rock, alternative rock and heavy metal.
00310823 Book/Online Audio $17.99

ROCK 'N' ROLL PIANO
by Andy Vinter
Take your place alongside Fats Domino, Jerry Lee Lewis, Little Richard, and other legendary players of the '50s and '60s! This book/audio pack covers: left-hand patterns; basic rock 'n' roll progressions; right-hand techniques; straight eighths vs. swing eighths; glisses, crushed notes, rolls, note clusters and more. Includes six complete tunes.
00310912 Book/Online Audio $18.99

SALSA PIANO
by Hector Martignon
From traditional Cuban music to the more modern Puerto Rican and New York styles, you'll learn the all-important rhythmic patterns of salsa and how to apply them to the piano. The book provides historical, geographical and cultural background info, and the 50+-tracks includes piano examples and a full salsa band percussion section.
00311049 Book/Online Audio $19.99

SMOOTH JAZZ PIANO
by Mark Harrison
Learn the skills you need to play smooth jazz piano – the theory, the tools, and the tricks used by the pros. Topics covered include: scales and chords; harmony and voicings; progressions and comping; rhythmic concepts; melodies and soloing; characteristic stylings; discussions on jazz evolution.
00311095 Book/Online Audio $19.99

STRIDE & SWING PIANO
by John Valerio
Learn the styles of the stride and swing piano masters, such as Scott Joplin, Jimmy Yancey, Pete Johnson, Jelly Roll Morton, James P. Johnson, Fats Waller, Teddy Wilson, and Art Tatum. This book/audio pack covers classic ragtime, early blues and boogie woogie, New Orleans jazz and more. Includes 14 songs.
00310882 Book/Online Audio $19.99

WORSHIP PIANO
by Bob Kauflin
From chord inversions to color tones, from rhythmic patterns to the Nashville Numbering System, you'll learn the tools and techniques needed to play piano or keyboard in a modern worship setting.
00311425 Book/Online Audio $17.99

HAL•LEONARD®

Prices, contents, and availability
subject to change without notice.

www.halleonard.com